THE GUMBY GANG ON HOLIDAY

'Right then,' said Steve. 'The meeting will now continue. Item one – what shall we do at Winchingsea?'

'Have fun,' said Howie.

'Have adventures,' said D

'Have sweets,'

'And hel vour?'

It was un

Things do the Gumby d, but they manage to f their ambitions in this series of hilarious holiday adventures.

Also by the same author, and available in Knight Books:

THE ADVENTURES OF THE GUMBY GANG
THE GUMBY GANG AGAIN
MORE ABOUT THE GUMBY GANG

The Gumby Gang on Holiday

Pamela Oldfield

Illustrated by Lesley Smith

KNIGHT BOOKS
Hodder and Stoughton

For Mabel and Norman

First published 1980 by Blackie & Son Ltd
Knight Books edition 1983

British Library C.I.P.

Oldfield, Pamela
The Gumby gang on holiday.
I. Title
823'.914[J] PZ7

ISBN 0 340 28561 3

The characters and situations in this book are entirely imaginary and bear no relation to any real person or actual happening

Printed and bound in Great Britain for Hodder and Stoughton Paperbacks, a division of Hodder and Stoughton Ltd., Mill Road, Dunton Green, Sevenoaks, Kent (Editorial Office: 47 Bedford Square, London, WC1 3DP) by Cox & Wyman Ltd, Reading

Contents

THE GANG GOES TO WINCHINGSEA

The train gave a jolt and they were off. The four children leaned out of the window and waved goodbye until the train rounded a bend. Their parents on the platform disappeared from view and the Gumby Gang settled themselves down and looked at each other.

"Do you think they're missing us?" asked Debbie.

Steve laughed. "We've only been gone half a minute!" he said. "How can they be missing us so soon?"

"I'm missing them," said Debbie, looking rather forlorn. It was the first time any of them had been away from home on their own. They were on their way to stay with Steve's grandmother who had rashly offered to have the four children and Buster for a whole week. She lived in a small village called Winchingsea and her cottage was only half a mile from the beach.

"I want to put my luggage on the rack," said Bet.

The luggage consisted of a duffel bag and Fido, a knitted rabbit.

"No one's stopping you," said Steve.

"But I can't reach the rack," she said.

"Ah," said Steve. "You want *me* to put your luggage in the rack." He tossed up the duffel bag and threw the rabbit up beside it, while the others watched admiringly. He was tall for his age and growing fast. "Any more for any more?" he asked.

"I'm keeping mine on my lap," said Debbie, "because it's full of important things."

"Such as?" said Howie.

"Such as my pocket money – and the Gumby Gang's notebook," said Debbie.

"I know," said Steve, "let's have a

meeting now to plan the holiday so we don't waste any time when we get down there."

It was agreed. There were no other passengers in the carriage so they were able to make themselves comfortable.

"Pull down the blinds," said Howie, "then no one can look in."

So they pulled down the blinds and the meeting began.

"Cauliflower," said Steve.

"Ditto," said Howie.

"Cauliflower cheese," said Bet.

Steve glared. "The meeting will not commence," he said, "until everyone says the password properly. 'Ditto' is not the password and neither is cauliflower cheese."

Howie opened his mouth to argue then changed his mind and said 'cauliflower'.

"Cauliflower cheese without the cheese," said Bet.

"I knew it!" said Steve. "I knew we shouldn't have let her join the Gang. She can't even say the password properly."

"I did say it," said Bet. "I said—"

While they were arguing, the door opened and a lady looked in.

"Why are these blinds down?" she asked in a frosty voice.

They all looked at Steve who was the leader of the Gang.

"Er—it's to keep people out," he said, "—because of the infection."

"Infection?" she said, looking startled. "What sort of infection?"

"It's Bet," said Steve. "She's got the measles."

The lady peered closely at Bet who smiled winningly and then remembered she had the measles and tried to look ill.

"I don't see any spots," she said.

"They're under my vest," said Bet. "Shall I show you?"

"No, thank you," the lady said hastily and withdrew, closing the door firmly behind her.

"That was a lie," said Debbie.

"It sure was," Howie agreed. "It sure was a whopping lie."

"How do you know for sure?" said Steve. "She might have the measles for all we know. She might have caught it just before we got on the train."

"We're stopping," Bet interrupted him. "Are we there?"

"Of course we're not," said Debbie. "The journey takes an hour."

The door opened and a man got in with a large suitcase. He swung it up into the rack, right on top of Fido! Bet let out a squeal of rage and the Gang looked at each other in dismay. He was a large man and he didn't look very friendly.

"Ask him!" Debbie whispered to Steve.

"You ask him," hissed Steve.

The man glanced at his watch, then took out a book and began to read.

"My p-poor Fido!" said Bet, bursting into tears. "He's all s-squashed and horrible. I want him. I want him. I—"

"Don't cry," said Debbie. "I'll get him for you." She cleared her throat. "Excuse me," she said to the man. "Your suitcase is on top of my sister's rabbit. Would you please move it and let us have him back?"

To her surprise the man took no notice at all. Debbie looked at Steve while Bet sobbed louder than ever.

"Perhaps he's deaf," said Steve. "Excuse me," he said loudly. "Could we have our rabbit, please? It's underneath your suitcase."

Still the man took no notice. Bet stopped crying suddenly and stood up and stamped on his foot.

"I want my rabbit!" she shouted. "I want my rabbit!"

The man was so surprised that he dropped his book and began to gabble away in a foreign language.

"Oh no!" gasped Steve. "He's French. He probably doesn't understand what we've been saying. And now Bet's trodden on his foot!"

They all began to wave their arms about, explaining to the poor man that it was a mistake and they were terribly sorry. It wasn't easy because they didn't know much French and the man looked very nervous. Buster joined in, barking furiously and leaping about over everybody. As soon as the train stopped at the next station, the man pulled down his suit-

case and jumped out. Steve gave Bet her rabbit and they all sat very quietly, thinking.

"It's your fault," grumbled Steve, scowling at Bet. "All that fuss about a stupid old rabbit."

"My rabbit is not stupid!" cried Bet. "He's got more brains than you."

"Don't be cheeky to the leader of the Gang," said Steve, "or you'll be thrown out of the meeting."

"Stupid old meeting! I'll throw myself out," said Bet crossly and before anyone could stop her she jumped out of the train, walked back along the platform and climbed into the next carriage.

"Let her go," said Steve. "We'll have the meeting without her."

Debbie was rather worried, but Howie said, "She'll be OK. We'll collect her when we get to Winchingsea."

So the meeting started with Steve announcing: "Item one—decide what to do on holiday. Any ideas?" he asked.

At that moment the train gave a shudder and there was a great jolt and a

clanging noise.

"We've hit something!" shouted Debbie but Steve pointed out that the train was still in the station. An announcement came over the loudspeaker and they all listened to it.

"The train now standing at platform one will divide. The front two coaches will call at Sunning, Merryton, Charkworth and—" The rest was rather garbled as a loud crackling came over the loudspeaker. The children looked at each other in alarm.

"Oh dear," said Debbie. "I wonder if Bet's in our half of the train. She'll be left behind. Quick. We must rescue her."

She put her head out of the window and shouted to the porter.

"Stop the train! My sister's back there. She's in the wrong coach. We're going to Winchingsea," she told him.

"Going to Winchingsea, are you?" He laughed. "Then it's *you* that's in the wrong coach. This one's going to Brighton. Hurry up and move yourselves. The driver's waiting to go."

Hurriedly Steve pulled down Bet's duffel bag and they all clambered out and rushed along the platform to find Bet.

She was sitting alone with Fido beside her. The guard slammed the door, blew his whistle and they were off once more. Buster settled himself under the seat and fell asleep and the Gumby Gang sorted themselves out.

"Right then," said Steve. "The meeting will now continue. Item one—what shall we do at Winchingsea?"

"Have fun," said Howie.

"Have adventures," said Debbie.

"Have sweets," said Bet hopefully.

"And help people," said Steve. "So all in favour?"

It was unanimous!

BUSTER'S DAY OUT

"Buster is going to love the beach," said Debbie happily. "He can swim in the sea—"

"And play with the ball," said Bet who carried an old tennis ball for the purpose.

"I expect he'll find another dog to play with," said Steve.

"He sure is going to have fun," said Howie and Buster, knowing that they were talking about him, ran round them in circles, barking his delight.

The Gumby Gang were on their way to the beach for a swim.

They had all said 'parsnips'—even Bet—and they were now hoping for fun and adventure. They took it in turns to carry the old haversack which contained the sandwiches and a flask of coffee plus a bottle of water and a bone for Buster. The sun was shining and the lane was full of eager children heading towards the beach with buckets and spades.

"The first thing I shall do," said Steve, "is to run along the breakwater and dive in."

"All your clothes will get wet," said Bet.

"I shall take them off first," said Steve.

"But you said the first thing you'd do—"

"Don't argue, Bet," said Debbie hastily. "You know what Steve means. You're just being awkward."

"I wish I had an aqualung," said Howie. "I'd swim around looking at all the tropical fish."

"Tropical fish?" said Steve. "In Winchingsea? You'll be lucky to see a crab. The water's always sandy and you can't see a thing . . . I wonder what Gran put in the sandwiches?"

"Cheese and pickle," said Debbie, "and egg and lettuce. I know because I helped her make them."

"Ugh!" said Steve. "I don't fancy them!"

"Don't eat them then," said Debbie. "All the more for the rest of us. Maybe Buster will let you share his bone."

Squabbling happily, they reached the beach, and found a space. In no time they were in their swimsuits and rushing into the water. As Steve had warned, it was fairly rough and milky brown with sand. Debbie began to screech as soon as it lapped her ankles.

"Oh, it's freezing! It's awful. I can't even feel my feet. They must be blue with cold!"

"Save you wearing socks," said Steve. He splashed past her and, plunging underneath the water, came up gasping for air and shivering. "It's OK when you get used to it," he said.

Bet paddled around in the shallow water and Howie sat down in it, shrieking horribly that it was too cold. It was all too much for poor Buster who had never in his life seen so much water or so many people. He was amazed to see the children submerging themselves in the water. Convinced that they were in terrible danger, he began to bark.

"Quit that barking, Buster," cried Howie. "We're OK. We're not drowning or anything."

But Buster was still not happy and tried desperately to reach them. He ran forward every time the waves receded and leaped back nervously when they turned again. And all the time he barked furiously until heads began to turn and people began to grumble.

"Can't you keep your dog quiet?" demanded a young man in glasses.

"It's deafening."

Debbie went rather pink. "I'll try," she said. Scrambling out of the water she was met by Buster who barked a greeting which was even noisier than before.

"Ssh! Silly boy," she said. "Why can't you behave like all the other dogs? They're not making such an exhibition. Now sit!"

Buster put his head on one side as though she had gone suddenly crazy.

"I mean it," she said sternly. "Sit!

That's better. And don't move."

He sat subdued as she marched back into the water, then he dropped down miserably on the sand.

"Wow!" said Howie admiringly. "You sure fixed him."

"It's nothing," said Debbie. "He just needs a firm hand."

After that Buster was quiet . . . very quiet!

"He's too quiet," said Steve ten minutes later. "Go and have a look, Bet, and see what he's doing."

"He's probably asleep," said Debbie and they watched as Bet trotted up the beach to investigate. When she reached the dog she gave a squeal of horror.

"He's eaten the sandwiches!" she cried. "Oh, Buster, you bad, awful dog!"

Debbie, Steve and Howie ran up on to the sand and they all glared at Buster who was swallowing the last crust.

"Well," said Steve. "All I can say is thank goodness he doesn't like coffee!"

They looked at each other and the idea of Buster unscrewing the thermos flask set them all laughing.

"Let's not grumble at him," said Howie. "He sure is awful but he's only a dog. Dogs have very small brains."

"His must be the size of a pea!" said Steve. "But we'll give him another chance. Let's have a cup of coffee to warm ourselves up."

They sat down and Debbie poured a generous helping into the beaker and they drank a few mouthfuls. Then she screwed the top on again.

"I've got an idea," said Steve. "Maybe if Buster could swim with us he'd understand that we're not in danger. I vote we carry him into the water, then let him swim."

The others agreed and Steve and Howie staggered into the water carrying Buster between them, much to the amusement of everyone else on the beach. When the water reached their knees, they lowered Buster gently into it.

"Good boy," said Debbie. "Isn't the water lovely?"

Buster didn't think so. He gave her a

baleful look and set off, swimming frantically towards the beach.

"No!" cried Bet. "Come back, Buster. You'll like it."

But, ignoring her, the dog trotted out onto the sand and shook himself, spraying water all over an elderly couple who were sitting in their deckchairs, minding their own business.

"Oh no!" groaned Steve. "I can't bear it."

The elderly gentleman jumped to his feet and waved his arms at Buster to 'shoo' him away. Poor Buster was so surprised he sprang backwards and landed right in the middle of someone's picnic. His back leg went straight into a large meat pie and his tail spilled a jug of lemonade into someone's lap. There was pandemonium!

"My beautiful meat pie!"

"Get away, you horrible brute!"

"Get out of it!"

"Help!"

The Gumby Gang dared not look. It was so awful. Buster, frightened by all the noise, raced off in the opposite direction,

straight into a well-behaved Alsatian who was watching the drama with polite interest. There was a short, sharp scuffle.

"Quick!" cried Debbie. "We must rescue Buster or he'll be eaten alive. That dog's much bigger than him."

The children rushed out of the water. Piercing howls, screams and a fierce snapping filled the air as the two dogs whirled around the beach, scattering holidaymakers in all directions. Before the children could reach him, Buster broke free, streaked away along the beach and disappeared.

"He sure is travelling!" said Howie impressed.

"He's doing ninety miles an hour at least," said Debbie.

Bet burst into tears, declaring that they had lost Buster forever.

"Of course we haven't," said Debbie, not feeling too sure about it. "We must go after him."

It was a good time to go. Angry people were descending on them in dozens so they hastily packed up their belongings and set off running along the beach to find Buster.

They didn't find him. An hour later they gave up searching and went home to tell Steve's Gran the dreadful news.

"Buster?" she said, surprised. "Oh, he came home ages ago. He ran under the bed and wouldn't come out so I left him there."

They rushed upstairs and hauled Buster out from his hiding place. Then they stared at him in dismay. In his mouth he held a sandal which he had found on his travels along the beach.

"It's all chewed up," said Bet. "Ooh, you bad dog!"

Buster hurriedly returned to the shelter of the bed and the Gumby Gang went downstairs, thoughtfully.

"Let's not go on the beach tomorrow," said Steve and for once they were all agreed.

THE OLD CAR

Steve's grandmother was talking about old Mr Benny and the children were listening half-heartedly. It wasn't until she mentioned the car that anyone showed much interest.

"He still drives, you know," she told them. "Over eighty, he is and still drives around in his old car. He really is a marvellous old chap."

"What sort of old car?" asked Steve.

"Oh, it's a blue car," she said vaguely. "Light blue I think but so dirty you can hardly see the colour. He never seems to clean it but it still goes chugging on."

Ten minutes later the Gumby Gang were holding a meeting and Steve announced their 'good deed for the week'.

"We're going to clean old Mr Benny's car," he told them. "We'll do it secretly and he'll never know it was us."

Debbie considered the idea.

"Suppose he doesn't want it cleaned?" she said.

"Of course he will," said Steve. "Anyone would want their car cleaned. We'll do it with soapy water, like a car wash."

"We could polish it too," said Howie.

"I'll polish the wheels," said Bet and Debbie hurriedly decided to join them.

"I'll do the silver bits," she said. "The bumpers and the headlights and the door handles. Anything silver is my job."

"What about inside?" asked Bet, fired with enthusiasm. "We could clear out the sweet papers—"

"—and hoover the grit out of the carpet—"

"—and empty the ashtrays—"

Once the Gumby Gang had made up their minds there was no stopping them! They found out that Mr Benny lived in Wellborne Road and promptly at three o'clock they set off with a collection of cleaning materials and a bucket for the water. They asked a man the way to Wellborne Road but he shook his head.

"I reckon you mean Wilshaw Lane," he said. "I can't place a road called Wellborne . . ."

Sure enough, in Wilshaw Lane they saw an old car standing outside a cottage. It certainly was dirty. The paint had flaked away in places and grass grew around the wheels.

"It's terrible," said Debbie. "Your Gran was right, Steve."

Howie whistled. "It sure is awful dirty," he agreed. "The sooner we clean it up the better."

"P-poor Mr B-Benny," said Bet and her eyes filled with tears.

"Don't you start grizzling," said Steve quickly. "We don't want cry babies in the Gang. And anyway he won't be poor Mr Benny when we've cleaned the car. He'll be lucky Mr Benny."

Bet sniffed loudly but cheered up a little at his words. The four children looked carefully up and down the lane. The old cottage had faded curtains and stood apart from the others in the lane so they would not be overlooked.

"There's no sign of life," said Steve but just to make sure he knocked at the door. There was no answer and they all sighed with relief.

"Right then," said Steve. "Howie, pop down to the bottom of the hill and fill the bucket from the pond."

Howie hurried off and was soon back. They scooped out a few strands of pond weed and added some Fairy Liquid. It was decided they would all share the washing and they were soon hard at work splashing soapy water over the old car and chattering excitedly.

Debbie wrung out her cloth and dried the windows.

"It's ever so old inside," she said. "I wonder if the door is locked?"

She tried the handle and to their delight it opened, though it creaked a bit because the hinges were rusty.

"I bet this car's very valuable," said Steve. "Old cars are. They're called vin-

tage cars and people have special rallies for them."

The 'vintage' car finally stood gleaming and glittering for the Gang's inspection. The windscreen and windows were clean. The paintwork was as shiny as could be expected and Debbie's 'silver bits" shone with metal polish. The four children looked at it proudly.

"The Gumby Gang has done a good job," said Steve.

"There's only one thing," said Debbie. "This car's grey, not blue."

"Wow!" said Howie. "She's right. It sure is grey."

"Trust my Gran to get it all wrong," said Steve. "She got the name of the road wrong, too. I expect it's because she's getting old."

"We're wasting time," said Debbie impatiently. "We ought to tidy up the inside now before Mr Benny comes back."

Steve nodded. "OK. You kids do the inside while I check the engine."

"Check the engine?" echoed Debbie. "How can you check it? You don't know anything about engines."

"Well, that's all you know," said Steve and he lifted the bonnet and began to poke about inside the engine, muttering "Carburettor . . . Mmmm . . . pistons . . . fan belt . . . Mmm . . ." but nobody believed him.

Bet scrambled into the driver's seat and pretended to drive. She pressed the horn and it blared suddenly in Steve's right ear, making him jump and hit his head on the bonnet.

"Stop that, Bet!" he said crossly but she poked out her tongue and began to turn the steering wheel.

"Brrrm! Brrrm!" she cried. "Everyone out of the way!"

"You're not even moving," said Howie but then Bet pulled a lever and it was the handbrake. The car began to roll down the hill with Bet inside it! Steve leaped out from beneath the bonnet and Debbie fell on to the grass screaming.

"Help! Help! Stop the car! Bet'll be killed!"

But there was nothing any of them could

do. The car rolled faster and faster with Bet inside it shouting "Whoa!" as though it was a horse. It swerved into the middle of the road, then swerved back again and finally ran off the road and into the hedge where it came to rest with a shuddering crash. One of the headlamps fell off and the back doors swung open. Steve, Howie and Debbie raced towards it as Bet tumbled out, grinning.

"Did you see me driving?" she demanded. "I really was. I was driving it."

The rest of the Gang surveyed the car in horrified silence.

"You've wrecked it," said Debbie in a shaky voice. "We shall all get into the most terrible trouble. We might even go to prison for ever!"

Howie opened his mouth to say "Wow" but changed his mind. He picked up the broken headlamp instead and handed it to Steve. Steve tried to fix it back on again but it wouldn't go.

"Who's going to tell?" asked Debbie.

"I will," said Steve, "because I'm the

leader of the Gang. I'll say it was an accident."

They all thought he was very brave. They collected their cleaning materials and walked slowly home.

An old blue car stood outside Gran's cottage and an old man stood at the gate chatting to her. She waved cheerfully as they appeared.

"Come and say 'Hello' to Mr Benny," she called. "This is my grandson, Steve," she explained, " and these are his friends . . . Well, say 'Hello' to Mr Benny. What's got into you all? You look as though you've seen a ghost."

They said 'Hello' and continued to gaze at the old car. The same thought was in all their minds. If this was Mr Benny's car, whose car had Bet driven into the hedge?

Later on when they confessed to Gran it all became clear. It seemed that the old grey car had been abandoned years ago but no one had bothered to move it. Gran telephoned the local garage and told them what had happened. They went round to collect it and sold it the same afternoon to a scrapyard. Everyone was well satisfied. The Gumby Gang cheered up again in no time. As Gran said, "It could have been a lot worse!"

THE GANG PLAYS TENNIS

"Tomato," said Howie. He helped himself to cornflakes and poured on a generous helping of milk.

"Tomato," said Steve, "and don't take all the milk. You've got enough there to float a battleship."

"A tomato is not a vegetable," said Debbie. "My teacher says it's a fruit so it can't be the password."

"Of course it's not a fruit," said Steve. "I mean, you can't have tomatoes and custard."

Ever loyal to her sister, Bet said, "Yes, you can. Tomatoes and custard is lovely."

"Ugh." Howie pulled a horrible face.

Steve was just threatening to give her some for pudding later in the day when his grandmother came into the room.

"Why don't you go down to the recreation ground?" she said. "They've got slides and swings—"

Steve rolled his eyes in mock horror. "Those are for kids," he said. "The Gumby Gang is not for playing on roundabouts with a lot of toddlers. Honestly, Gran!"

"Sorry, I'm sure," she said, laughing. "What about the tennis court? You might get an hour's tennis if you go down early enough."

Steve's eyes gleamed. "Tennis!" he said. "Now tennis would be super—but we haven't got any rackets."

"I'll find you a couple," said Gran, "and I think Mrs Dennis next door also has one. Pop round, Steve, and ask her nicely if you can borrow it."

"That's only three," said Bet, "so I bags be the ball-boy because I don't like tennis."

"How d'you know?" asked Howie. "I

bet you've never even played it."

"I haven't," said Bet, "but that's because I don't like it."

Howie looked puzzled and decided to concentrate on the last few cornflakes in his bowl.

Half an hour later the Gumby Gang were on their way with three tennis rackets and four balls and fifty pence.

"We can either play one against one, while one sits out," said Steve, "or we can play two against one."

"Two against one!" said Debbie. "Howie and me against you because you're older than us and you've got longer arms."

They skirted round the children in the playground and found the tennis court deserted. There was a hut with a small elderly man in it. He was the keeper and he took their fifty pence and gave them a ticket.

"One hour only," he said grimly. "That is sixty minutes, and not a minute more."

They looked at him.

"We know that," said Debbie indignantly. "Everyone knows that sixty minutes make one hour."

"Sixty seconds make a minute," began Bet, "sixty minutes make an hour, twenty-four hours make one day, seven days—"

"Thank you but I do know my arithmetic," said the keeper, looking grimmer than ever. "I'm not as dumb as I look."

"Thank goodness for that!" whispered Steve and they all giggled.

As they walked towards the centre of the court, he raised his voice and shouted: "Sixty, remember. Not sixty-one. Sixty."

"Gee!" said Howie. "What a crum bum!"

But they soon forgot him in the excitement of their first game of tennis. Steve stood at one end of the court and Debbie and Howie at the other.

"I'll serve first," said Steve. He threw up the ball, and took a terrific swing at it with the racket. To everyone's amazement he hit it and it whizzed across the net at such a speed that Debbie and Howie ducked.

"Steve's won," said Bet and she clapped politely.

"He has not won!" said Debbie crossly. "He ought to be disqualified. He's dangerous. And anyway it was outside the line, so there."

Undismayed, Steve then threw up three balls, one after the other and missed them all.

"The net's too high," said Steve. "Ball-boy, lower the net please. You'll find a handle on the post. Just turn it until I say 'stop'."

But Bet got carried away. She liked turning the handle so she ignored Steve and soon had the net about twelve inches from the ground!

"Now try," said Debbie, trying not to laugh.

"Very funny," said Steve. "Wind it up again, ball-boy or *you* will be disqualified."

"You didn't say 'please'," said Bet. "My Mum says you should—"

"PLEASE!" roared Steve and Bet hastily wound it back to its previous height.

"Stop!" cried Steve and was ready to serve again. This time he managed to hit the ball but it bounced midway between

Debbie and Howie. They both ran for it, missed and hit each other!

"Ouch!"

"Ooh, gosh!"

They glared at each other, Debbie rubbing her ankle and Howie rubbing his lower arm.

"You're supposed to hit the ball, not each other," said Steve.

"Oh, you are a smarty boots today," said Debbie. "Well, I think it's *my* turn to serve so let's see if you can hit it."

After a brief argument, Steve tossed over the balls.

"On your marks—" shouted Bet. "Get set!"

"This isn't a race, Bet," said Debbie. "You don't have to say that."

"I want to say it."

"Well you can't."

Debbie threw up the ball, hit it—and they all watched it land in the right place and bounce up again—right through a hole in the netting that surrounded the court. It fell into some long grass and they wasted nearly ten minutes trying to

find it.

"Never mind," said Steve. "We've still got three balls left."

But not for long. Debbie's next attempt was underarm and she sent the ball over the top of the netting, where it bounced on the roof of the keeper's hut and disappeared across the playground. The third ball had a split in it and wouldn't bounce at all.

"My turn," said Howie, suddenly aware that if he didn't hurry up there would be no balls left. He threw up the ball and hit it into the right court. Steve was so surprised he just let it go past him.

"Howie's won!" shouted Bet.

"I haven't," said Howie. "It's fifteen-love."

They all stared at him, astonished.

"I didn't know you could score," said Debbie. "Why didn't you say so before?"

"I guess no one asked me," said Howie. "My Pop taught me. My Pop is the best tennis player in the States. Why, my Pop—"

They all groaned.

"Serve again, Howie," said Debbie hastily. "Serve one to me."

He did and Debbie hit it back! Howie missed it.

"Fifteen all!" cried Steve. "Well done, Gang. Now you're getting the right idea."

It seemed that Howie really could play tennis and it was decided that Debbie and Steve should play together against him to make a more even game. They were soon rallying quite well and Bet was kept busy running about after the only remaining ball. That is, until she was accidentally hit on the head by it and went into a sulk and wouldn't be ball-boy any longer.

"I'll be ball-boy, then," said Debbie. "You come and have a go, Bet, you'll like it."

But before Bet could say 'No' the old man appeared at the gate, tapping his watch.

"Sixty-two and a half minutes!" he told them. "I knew you'd be up to something if I didn't keep an eye on you. Sixty-three, now . . . Sixty-three and a half . . ."

They left him to it and walked slowly

back through the park.

"Why does that man keep counting?" Bet asked.

"Just to prove he can, I suppose," said Debbie. "Perhaps he thinks it's a sign of great intelligence."

"If he's so intelligent, why is he a park keeper?" said Steve. "He should have been a brain surgeon."

"He's not tall enough," said Bet.

"Short men can be brain surgeons," said Debbie.

"But how do they reach people's brains?" asked Bet and the others burst out laughing. Howie, being a show-off, clutched at his stomach and staggered about.

"I guess they use a ladder!" he suggested and they rolled about on the grass, laughing until the tears rolled down their cheeks.

All, that is, except Bet, who didn't understand the joke and wondered about it all the way home.

THE VILLAGE FÊTE

Steve's grandmother was busy making scones. Forty-eight scones, to be precise.

"We'll never eat all these," said Bet, surprised, but Gran explained that they were to sell at the village fête.

"There'll be a cake stall," she said, "and a stall selling bottles—"

"Empty bottles?" asked Howie.

"No. Full bottles—of pickle or jam or hand-cream. Anything that comes in a bottle. There'll be a raffle and a jumble sale and a dog show—"

"A dog show!" cried Steve. "Why didn't you tell us before?"

Debbie stared at him.

"You're not going to put Buster in, are you?" she said. "I mean, he's a nothing-special dog. He's not an Alsatian."

"Or a Poodle," said Howie.

"Or a Red Setter," said Debbie.

"Or an elephant," said Bet helpfully.

They ignored her.

"He could go in the class for mongrels," said Gran. "He is quite intelligent."

"Is he?" said Debbie and they looked at Buster who was sprawled on the rug, eyes rolling, tongue hanging out of his mouth.

"He looks kinda crazy," said Howie doubtfully. "Do they have a class for crazy dogs?"

"Perhaps he could win the prize for craziest dog," said Debbie.

Buster took exception to their lack of respect and took himself off into the garden with baleful looks in all directions. Steve sighed.

"We'll try," he said. "We'll clean him up a bit. Come on."

There wasn't much time but the four children did what they could.

Bet took off Buster's collar and gave it a good polish. Steve found an old toothbrush and cleaned his teeth.

"The judges always look at their teeth," he said.

Debbie brushed him thoroughly and Howie washed his paws and dried them carefully on a cloth.

Then they stood round, examined him critically and decided he was ready.

"So off we go," said Gran, who had packed the scones into a large cardboard box. And off they went.

Winchingsea village hall was decked out in coloured bunting and already a queue was forming outside. The Gumby Gang and Buster followed Gran to a side door. On the grass at the rear of the hall various competitions were being arranged and people scurried about looking anxiously at their watches.

"You'd better not bring Buster into the hall," Gran told Steve. "He's so big and bouncy. Take him under a shady tree and keep him clean for the dog show."

Steve did as she suggested and Howie, Debbie and Bet went into the hall with her. At once a large lady with white hair rushed up.

"Oh, dear," she wailed. "Mrs Green has hurt her leg and can't come and who is to take over the jumble stall? Mrs Jones is on the bottle stall and . . ."

"The children will help. Don't worry any more," said Gran cheerfully. "Debbie and Howie can run the cake stall and I'll do the jumble."

The large lady looked at Debbie and Howie. "Are you sure they can manage?" she asked.

"Quite sure," said Gran briskly, and in no time at all the two children were installed behind the trestle table. There they found a pile of paper bags in which to put the cakes and a saucer in which to put the money.

"There's already some money," Howie told Debbie.

Gran explained that the fivepenny pieces and pennies were change for the people who didn't have the exact money for the cakes. For a while no one noticed that Bet was scowling horribly but when she began to stamp her foot, they did.

"Oh dear," said Debbie but it was too late. Bet burst into tears.

"I w-want to help!" she wailed. "I want t-to be on a stall. I want to. I want—"

"Ssh," said Debbie hurriedly. "Everyone's looking at you."

"Don't c-care," sobbed Bet. "It's not f-fair. I'm in the G-Gang, too, so I w-want to help."

"She can sell some raffle tickets," said Gran. "It's quite easy." She produced a large box from behind the counter. In it was a beautifully dressed doll. Bet's tears vanished like water down a drain.

"The tickets are two for fivepence," Gran told her. "You are too young to give change, so if the people haven't got fivepence ask them to come back later when they have. Do you understand?"

Bet nodded. "Two tickets for fivepence."

They set the doll on a spare chair and Bet sat beside it on another. Gran returned to the jumble stall and at last it was two o'clock. The doors opened and the hall was immediately filled with the sound of rushing feet and eager voices. Debbie and Howie waited nervously as a small crowd collected round the cake stall.

"I'll take the chocolate cake," said one woman and Debbie looked at the ticket.

"Fifty pence, please," she told her and carefully slipped the cake into a bag.

"A dozen scones, please," said another woman and Howie made a quick calculation in his head. Twelve scones at threepence each . . . "Thirty-six pence, please," he said and the woman counted out the money.

"The lemon sponge, dear, please."

"Half a dozen sausage rolls."

"The cherry cake and six mince pies."

It was hard work!

Above the sound of the voices and feet they suddenly heard Bet's voice loud and clear.

"Only fivepence for two tickets! Only fivepence! Thank you. Two tickets, thank you."

Debbie grinned at Howie.

"Listen to Bet," said Debbie. "She's awfully good at it."

"She sure is enjoying herself," said Howie.

"Four jam tarts, four scones and the swiss roll—"

Howie reached hastily for another paper bag.

"Would you put the coffee gateau by for me?" asked a lady. "I'll come back for it in ten minutes."

Debbie nodded and put the gateau behind her on the chair.

"We'll soon be sold out," said Howie. "Then we can go and watch the dog show."

Across the room they could see Steve's grandmother busy at the jumble stall. Old jumpers, shoes and coats were eagerly snapped up and carried away. Suddenly, above the hubbub they heard Bet's voice.

"You gave me fivepence and I gave you two tickets."

Then a man's voice. "But you gave me two the same! I want my money back."

"Well you can't have it!" cried Bet shrilly and Debbie groaned.

"Oh lord, now what's happened?" she

said. "You look after the cakes, Howie, and I'll go and take a look."

By the time she reached her little sister there were several people waving green tickets and complaining in loud voices.

"I'm her sister," said Debbie. "What's happened?"

"I gave them two tickets!" shouted Bet. "I *did*!"

"Your sister gave everyone two tickets," said one of the men, "But the numbers are the same. I've got two number nines."

"And I've got two seventeens."

"You see," said Bet triumphantly. "They've got two numbers each."

Fortunately Gran arrived to sort out the muddle. Bet had given them two identical numbers instead of keeping one of each pair to go into the hat! An announcement was made over the loudspeaker. Everyone who had bought tickets for the doll was asked to return them and two new numbers were given to them. It was all most unfortunate.

"Don't blame me," said Bet five minutes later as she sucked an ice lolly.

"Gran didn't say give different numbers. She said—"

"Oh do stop going on about it," said Debbie and she led the unrepentant Bet back to the cake stall. As they reached it Howie was wrapping up the last cake and Debbie flopped thankfully onto the chair. There was a horrible squelching noise and her mouth dropped open in horror. When she stood up most of the coffee gateau was stuck to the back of her skirt!

"Ugh!" said Howie. "That sure looks awful."

Debbie twisted round and tried to see how bad it was. At that moment the lady who had bought it arrived to collect it and smiled cheerfully at the two children.

"I've come for my gateau," she reminded them.

Debbie opened her mouth and shut it again without saying anything.

The woman looked at Howie.

"It's gone," he said.

"Gone?" she repeated. "Gone where? It was on that—Oh!"

The sentence ended in a small scream

as she looked at the chair and saw the flattened mess that had once been a gateau.

"What happened?" she asked faintly.

"Something sat on it," said Debbie.

"What sort of something?"

"Me," said Debbie and she turned slowly round to reveal the rest of the gateau.

They had to give back the money she had paid and she went away looking rather disgruntled. Howie set to and scraped off the cream with a plastic knife which happened to be handy.

"You looked kinda cute sitting in that cake," he told her and Debbie began to see the funny side of it. When they stopped laughing she said, "Let's go and watch the dog show. Maybe Buster will win a prize."

It didn't seem very likely. There were eight dogs in thc ring, all mongrels. Seven of them were sitting quietly. Buster was not. He was trying to scratch his left ear and Steve was trying to stop him because he didn't want the judge to think he had fleas.

Buster was getting very cross and when the judge reached him he was in no mood to be inspected. As soon as Steve tugged him to a standing position, he flopped down again. When the judge tried to look in his mouth he bit his hand—not very hard but enough to make him curse. Then, being a kindly dog at heart, he wagged his tail and leaped up at him to show that they were still friends. The judge staggered backwards and stepped on the tail of the dog behind him who squealed in protest. While the judge was apologising to the dog's owner, Steve dragged Buster out of the ring and joined Debbie, Howie and Bet.

"I've withdrawn him," he said. "I didn't like the judge."

"Neither did Buster," giggled Bet. "Let's go and find Gran."

On the way home they told Gran what a super afternoon they'd had.

"If you like, we'll come down and help at the next fête," said Steve.

Gran, who had heard all about the disasters, hid a smile and said, "Thank you."

THE GANG'S BIG ADVENTURE

"Why do we have to pick mushrooms," grumbled Bet. "I don't even like mushrooms and neither does Fido."

"How d'you know he doesn't?" asked Steve. "I bet you've never asked him."

Bet opened the carrier bag. The knitted rabbit lay at the bottom covered with mushrooms. She whispered into the bag and then smiled triumphantly.

"He says he doesn't," she said. "So there, clever clogs."

Howie, ignoring this back-chat, dived suddenly into a large patch of long grass and emerged with two more mushrooms.

"I'm getting awfully hungry," said

Debbie as he dropped them into the carrier bag. "Is it time to go home yet?"

Steve looked at his watch and for once it happened to be working.

"Nearly half past seven," he told her. "I should think we've picked enough. We might as well go home—if we can find that apology for a dog."

The four children looked hopefully in all directions. There was no sign of Buster but there was a lot of noise coming from a nearby dyke. They whistled but he didn't come.

"Perhaps he's swimming in the dyke," said Debbie but Howie reminded her that Buster didn't care for water.

They wandered over to the edge of the dyke and looked down. With horror they saw what Buster was barking at. A large sheep had slipped into the dyke and stood with only its head above water, rolling its eyes in fright.

"Oh, the poor thing!" cried Debbie and Bet burst into loud sobs.

"Clever dog to find it," said Steve, "but now you must be quiet. Do you understand? QUIET!"

And as leader of the Gumby Gang Steve now took charge of the rescue operation.

"Howie," he said. "You take Buster over there and make him be quiet. All that barking is scaring the sheep . . . Bet, stop boo-hooing and pick some grass to feed the sheep. That will distract it while Debbie and I wade out behind it and push it up onto the bank."

They all looked at him admiringly except Buster who was busily trying to nip Howie's hand as he tried to pull him away.

"Do we have to take our shoes off?" asked Debbie but Steve had already taken his off so she hurried to do the same. Bet rushed about tugging at the grass and when she had collected enough they were ready.

"Right—into action!" cried Steve and he and Debbie lowered themselves into the green water.

Debbie gave a little scream as the water reached her knees. "It's horrible!" she wailed. "All slimy and horrible."

"Ssh!" said Steve. "You'll upset the

sheep. Now, we'll work our way towards it—slowly."

Bet held out the grass and the sheep snatched at it greedily.

"Hurry up," said Bet. "Or it'll have eaten all the grass. It's a very greedy eater."

"Like you, then," muttered Steve but fortunately Bet didn't hear. As soon as they were in position he and Debbie caught hold of the sheep's woolly fleece and began to heave and push it towards the bank.

"Now Bet, catch hold of its neck," cried Steve. "You pull and we'll—ouch! The stupid ungrateful animal has trodden on my foot."

Bet giggled and Buster, suddenly wriggling free, came rushing over, barking furiously. The sheep, thoroughly upset, tossed its head and Bet lost her balance and fell into the water. Her scream became a gurgle as Howie arrived to hold out a helping hand.

"Don't bother to pull her out," said Steve. "Since she's already wet she might

as well help me and Debbie. This sheep is terribly heavy. Howie, keep Buster away, for Pete's sake!"

So Steve, Bet and Debbie struggled with the sheep until at last they managed to get its front legs on to dry land.

"Phew!" gasped Debbie as they stopped for a breath. "It's hard work but I think we're winning."

"Good job we came along," said Steve. "The poor thing might have drowned."

"Or starved to death," said Howie.

"Unless it ate a fish," said Bet.

"Sheep don't each fish," said Steve.

"How do you know?" asked Bet, trying to squeeze the water out of her curls. "My ribbon's all wet."

"It would be," said Steve.

A thought struck Debbie and her eyes glowed suddenly.

"Perhaps we'll get a medal," she said. "And our photograph in the paper. 'The Gumby Gang's Heroic Rescue'—or something."

"I expect we will," said Steve, wishing he had thought of it. "Perhaps we'll be on the radio."

"On the TV!" cried Howie. "I sure would like that."

They were all lost in a wonderful day-dream until finally Steve pulled himself together.

"Well, we'd better get the rest of this sheep on to dry land," he said. "I shouldn't think they'll give us any medal for rescuing half a sheep."

So they began to pull and tug again until at last the sheep was out of the water. It stood shivering while muddy water trickled from its thick curly fleece. The Gumby Gang looked at it proudly.

"Four children risk their lives to save sheep," said Steve, "or 'Race Against Time in Rescue Bid'."

"We ought to rub it dry," said Debbie. "It might catch a chill."

Steve laughed. "Of course it won't," he said. "Sheep get wet when it rains. They don't mind at all."

"I mind," said Bet, "and I might catch a chill."

"She's right," said Debbie. "We'd better go home and tell your Gran what happened. Where are the mushrooms?"

Howie picked up the carrier bag but Steve hesitated.

"How are we going to have our picture in the paper," he said, "if no one is here to photograph us?"

"I don't know," said Debbie, "but we can't just hang about waiting for a photographer to come along. I mean, there's no one in sight except us."

"There sure is," said Howie, pointing excitedly.

They all stared hopefully towards a figure coming across the grass, but he carried a gun, not a camera.

"It must be the farmer," said Steve. "We'll tell him about rescuing his sheep and then he can tell the newspaper and they can—"

But Buster, seeing an interesting stranger, began to bark and before they could quieten him the startled sheep leaped backwards. It fell into the dyke with a loud splash, bleating loudly. There was a roar from the approaching farmer and he ran towards them shaking his fist angrily.

"You kids get away from that sheep!" he shouted. "And take that dog with you."

The children stared at him open-mouthed, too amazed to defend themselves against the unexpected attack.

"Kids like you are a menace," he grumbled. "Why, a sheep could drown like that."

He waded into the water, grabbed the sheep and hauled it out single-handed. It ran off, shaking its head and looking very bewildered. The children tried to explain, all talking at once, but the farmer stamped away grumbling and muttering to himself.

"Well!" said Debbie and couldn't think of anything else to say.

"He didn't give us our medals," said Bet. "Perhaps he forgot."

"And perhaps he isn't going to," said Steve.

They walked slowly back to the gate and out into the lane.

No one spoke for a long time until Howie found half a packet of wine gums in his pocket.

"Don't give Bet one," said Steve. "She's only five and she might get drunk!"

Bet found this very funny. Howie gave them one each and they began to feel a little more cheerful.

"Keep your eyes open," said Debbie. "We might see something else that needs rescuing."

But fortunately they didn't.

FUN AT THE FAIR

"I wish we had brought Buster," said Debbie for the tenth time and Steve groaned.

"You can't take a dog to a fair," said Howie. "The noise would scare him."

"And what would he do?" said Steve. "I mean, a dog's a dog! Buster would look pretty silly riding in a dodgem car or trying to throw a ball at a coconut."

"Potato," said Bet.

They stared at her in surprise.

"You don't throw balls at potatoes," said Debbie, "it's coconuts. They put the coconuts on sticks and—"

"I mean potato," said Bet. "The password is potato and we haven't said it."

"We don't have to," said Steve. "We're

not having a meeting. We're going to the fair."

"But that's an adventure," Bet insisted, "and the Gumby Gang is for having adventures so we all ought to say potato."

"Well, we're not going to," said Steve.

"Potato," said Bet. "Potato, potato—"

She was still saying it when they reached the entrance to the field where the fair was being held. Inside all was music and lights and laughter. Debbie, Steve, Howie and Bet each clutched a fifty pence piece—a present from Gran. They looked at each other, eyes shining with excitement.

"Right then," said Steve. "In we go!"

And in they went. For the first ten minutes they wandered around just looking at everything. There was so much to see. It was not yet dark but all the stalls were lit with rows of coloured lights. There were hoopla stalls, darts, lucky numbers and bingo. There were dodgems, roundabouts and swings and a helter-skelter. There was a large structure with small chairs that swung round and round as they went up and over like a wheel. The children watched breathlessly as the occupants whirled past, screaming wildly.

"That contraption makes me feel sick just to look at it," said Debbie but Steve laughed.

"That's because you're a girl," he said loftily. "And it's not a contraption, it's called 'The Octopus' and I shall have a go on it later."

"So will I," said Bet.

"No you won't," said Debbie quickly, "because Mum said I'm to look after you and it's too dangerous."

They bought four toffee apples and moved on, chewing noisily and trying to decide what to spend their money on. Howie wanted to go on the dodgems. Debbie and Howie fancied their luck at darts and Steve wanted to try for a coconut. But they found themselves at the rifle range and suddenly everyone wanted to shoot.

"Look at all the prizes you can win," Steve gloated, pointing to an impressive array of ornaments, cameras and toys. Bet gasped.

"Look at that giant teddy," she whispered and her eyes gleamed. "That's what I'm going to win."

The rest of the Gang looked—and laughed.

The giant bear was the best prize of all and sat in the place of honour in the middle of the other prizes. It was bigger than Bet herself and its gleaming fur shone like gold. Round its neck was a large pink bow.

"I'll go first," said Steve, "and show you all how to do it."

They watched carefully as he paid his money and the lady gave him a rifle. He took his place next to a man with white hair and a large white moustache. Steve aimed the gun at the row of metal ducks which moved slowly past a painted background.

Bang!

"You missed," said Bet sweetly.

Bang!

"Missed again!" said Bet and Steve put down the rifle.

"No wonder," he said crossly, "with you standing right at my elbow. You're putting me off."

Bet took a large step backwards and Steve fired again. The ducks continued to slide slowly past.

"They go too fast," grumbled Steve. "No one could hit them at that speed."

"That man hits them," said Howie. "He hits them every time. He sure can shoot."

They all turned to watch the white-haired man beside them. He knocked down a duck whenever he fired. Bang! Bang! Down went two more ducks.

"Have another try, Steve," said Debbie kindly. "I expect he's had more practice than you."

Steve fired twice more and knocked down a duck. The lady gave him a small grey ticket and turned away.

"Hooray! I've done it!" he yelled, leaping about in his excitement. "I knew I could do it. Now, which prize shall I have?"

After much thought he decided on a camera.

"You haven't got enough tickets," said

the lady. Steve looked at her blankly. "You need a hundred tickets for the camera," she told Steve.

"A hundred!" said Steve. "But I've only got one."

"Try and get the rest then," she said.

Steve shook his head. "What can I have for one ticket?" he asked and she handed him a blue plastic egg cup.

"How many tickets do I need for the teddy?" Bet asked.

"Two hundred," she said and they all gasped with disbelief.

"That settles it," said Steve. "I'm not wasting any more money on the rifle range! Let's have a go on the dodgems instead!"

But Bet refused to abandon her teddy bear so they left her there, promising to collect her later. They shrieked their way round on the dodgems—Debbie and Howie in one car being chased by Steve in another. Then they went down the helter-skelter, close behind each other, and piled up in a heap at the bottom, giggling. The Hall of Mirrors was great fun, too. It was full of uneven mirrors that distorted people's reflections. Howie found himself with a very tall head and almost no legs.

"You look much better like that!" Steve told him humorously and then Howie and Debbie looked at Steve's reflection. He had long legs and a very wide head.

"I always said you were a fat-head!" said Debbie and ran away quickly to escape his wrath.

Finally, they stood under 'The Octopus' and Steve wondered whether to have a go or not.

"It looks very dangerous to me," said Debbie nervously. "You might fall out and kill yourself."

The three children watched as it slowed to a halt and people climbed out, thankful to be on firm ground again.

"Perhaps I won't bother," said Steve. "I've only got ten pence left and I'd like some candy floss."

"You're scared," said Howie. "You're scared to go on it."

"I am not scared!" said Steve. "But I bet you are."

"I sure am!" said Howie and Debbie agreed that she was, too.

"I'm not scared," said a voice and they turned to see the giant golden teddy bear standing behind them.

"That was Bet's voice," said Debbie, puzzled.

I'm here," said the teddy and Bet poked her head round the side of it.

"Bet!" cried Debbie. "What are you doing with that teddy? Take it back at once or you'll get into terrible trouble."

"I won't," said Bet. "It's mine."

Steve's eyes nearly popped out of his head. "You knocked down two hundred ducks! I don't believe it. You couldn't hit a football with a pea-shooter!"

Bet smiled her sweetest smile. "I call him Honey," she told them.

"Wow!" said Howie. "She sure must be a terrific shot."

There was a baffled silence. At that moment a white-haired man came towards them out of the crowd. It was the man who had been beside Steve at the rifle range.

200

"Is your little friend pleased with her bear?" he asked. "I've no children of my own and I know she wanted it."

Bet went rather pink.

"You mean she didn't win it?" said Steve and the man laughed and shook his head.

"I want to go on 'The Octopus'," said Bet, to change the subject, "and so does Honey. Come on Steve."

"I haven't got enough money," said Steve quickly but Bet said she hadn't spent all hers and would pay for him. So he had to go.

He and Bet and the giant teddy bear squeezed into a double seat, the music started and off they went. Slowly at first up and up, round and round. As it went faster Bet began to shriek with excitement and she waved to Debbie and Howie as she swung past.

"I wish she wouldn't do that," said Debbie. "She should hold on with both hands."

"She'll fall," said Howie. "She'll come crashing down like a—"

"Do you mind!" said Debbie.

The white-haired man beside them smiled at Debbie.

"Don't worry," he said. "They look dangerous but they're really quite safe."

As he uttered the word 'safe' there was a shrill scream from Bet and the crowd stared aghast as something hurtled downwards.

"Bet!" cried Debbie—but it was the giant teddy bear and it fell right on top of the man with white hair and knocked him flat on his back. There was a great commotion as everyone rushed to pick him up and dust him down.

"Are you hurt?" asked Debbie shakily and was relieved to see him smile.

"No bones broken," he said. "But I was wrong about 'The Octopus'. It certainly is dangerous!"

"It's not 'The Octopus' that's dangerous," said Steve. "It's Bet. She's a menace."

The machine stopped and Bet came rushing up to see if Honey was safe. She received a short sharp lecture from Steve

and for once in her life managed to look rather downhearted. But the white-haired man was very kind. He said it was an accident and bought them each some candy floss and then it was time to go.

"Shall we come again next year?" said Bet. "We might see that nice man again—the one with white hair."

"With you in the Gang," said Steve, "I shall probably have white hair myself," and Howie, Debbie and Bet giggled all the way home.

A PRESENT FOR GRAN

Debbie waited until they had all said 'marrow' and then she dropped her bombshell.

"We've spent all our money," she said, "and we haven't bought a present for Steve's Gran."

"Oh lord!" said Steve.

"I didn't know it was her birthday," said Howie. "I wonder how old she is. A hundred, I guess. She sure looks pretty old."

"Two hundred, I should think," said Bet wide-eyed at the thought of it. "Or three hundred."

"You're being stupid as usual," said Steve loftily. "My Gran, for your information, is only sixty-three—and anyway it isn't her birthday so it doesn't matter how old she is."

"Then why buy her a present?" asked Howie.

"Because we've been staying with her for a week," Debbie explained patiently. "It's a 'thank you' present for all her hard work—cooking and shopping."

At that moment Steve's grandmother put her head round the door.

"Do you children like weddings?" she asked. "Because if you do, young Sharon Kemp is getting married at ten o'clock and your train doesn't go until twelve."

"Yes we do," said Debbie and Bet.

"No we don't," said Howie and Steve.

Gran laughed. "Well, if you do decide to go and watch you've got ten minutes to get to the church. I'm going next door for a cup of coffee."

Five minutes later the Gumby Gang sat along the churchyard wall watching the guests arrive for the wedding. Some of the men wore smart grey suits and top hats and the women wore beautiful dresses and large floppy hats.

"They all look pretty silly to me," said Steve. "I mean, why are the men wearing those ridiculous hats?"

"I expect they're all important people," said Debbie, "or else very rich."

"Well I shan't wear a top hat when I get married," Steve said.

"Do you think someone will want to marry you then?" asked Bet, genuinely surprised, but she was promptly pushed off the wall by Steve who was not amused.

"Here comes the bride," said Debbie, helping her up again. "Oh, I'm going to wear a dress like that!"

"So am I," said Bet and she stood up on the wall so she could see better.

The bride's dress was of white lace and she wore a long veil which floated behind her as she walked along. Her bouquet was of yellow roses and the four little bridesmaids wore blue.

As soon as they were all in the church the Gumby Gang returned to the problem of Gran's present.

"Maybe we could make her something," Howie suggested as they wandered through the churchyard and out into the lane.

"Such as?" said Debbie.

"I guess I'm good at woodwork," he told them modestly. "I could make something out of wood."

"But what?" asked Steve.

"She's always wanted a rocking chair," said Debbie. "She said so last night."

"Brilliant," said Steve sarcastically. "Howie's got no wood and no tools and we're going home in an hour. He couldn't even make a matchbox let alone a rocking chair!"

Debbie went all huffy, and Howie said, "Well, have you got any better ideas?" but he hadn't. Bet said, "I'm going to give her these," and held out a bunch of pink carnations for their inspection.

"Where did you find those?" Debbie asked.

Bet waved her hand vaguely towards the churchyard.

"There are flowers all over the place," she said, "but these were the best ones."

Steve closed his eyes and groaned.

"She's taken them from one of the graves!" he said. "She's stolen them. I knew she should never have joined the Gang. She'll get us a bad name."

"You must put them back, Bet," said Debbie. "At once."

There was a short sharp argument in which Bet screamed and stamped her feet and said 'No' and Steve shook her and said 'Yes'. Howie watched with his fingers in his ears until it was over.

They marched Bet back into the churchyard and returned the flowers to their vase with a sigh of relief that no one had seen them. Debbie arranged the flowers carefully and the Gang tiptoed away again.

"But it's given me an idea," said Steve, when they were once more in the lane. "We'll pick a bunch of wild flowers for Gran—"

"And tie them round with one of Bet's ribbons," said Debbie. "That's a marvellous idea."

"We could send her a card," suggested Howie, "and all sign it with GG after each name."

"Gee gee?" said Bet. "What's it got to do with horses?"

"Not gee gee," said Howie. "G . . . G . . . for Gumby Gang. Then she will wonder what the letters stand for—"

"But we won't tell," said Debbie, "because the Gang is secret and it will remain a mystery! What do you think, Steve?"

"It's a good idea," he said, "except that we haven't got a card and we've no money to buy one."

"We'll make one then,' said Debbie. "We'll find a piece of card and draw flowers and things."

They found some foxgloves, some cow parsley and a dogrose and then turned back. On the way home they passed the church again. The photographer was busy arranging the bridal group outside the porch. He was a small tubby man with a permanent smile and he bustled about, pushing and pulling people into place. As they watched he stood back, satisfied.

"Aha, I think we've got it at last," he

told them cheerfully. "So let's have some radiant smiles please, ladies and gents. Some really radiant smiles! This is a happy, happy day and I want you all to look absolutely radiant!"

Steve nudged Debbie and Howie and they looked at Bet who was smiling as radiantly as she could.

"Not you, silly," he said. "You're not in the photograph."

She stopped smiling and put out her tongue and said, "Pig," and Debbie said, "Don't swear, Bet."

Click.

"And just one more, please," cried the photographer.

Click.

They watched as he began to arrange the next group. This was a much larger one, it seemed.

"Any aunts or uncles, please," he shouted. "Aunts and uncles of the bride and groom, please. That's splendid. Absolutely splendid. Now, any cousins?"

"It's beginning to look like a football crowd," said Steve, "and look at that

awful child at the front there, pushing in. She's grinning like a loony!"

They all looked.

"She looks a bit like you, Bet," said Debbie, "smiling radiantly."

They looked round for Bet and she wasn't there! They looked again at the child in the wedding group and gasped with horror.

"It *is* Bet!" cried Debbie.

The photographer stepped back and surveyed the group.

"One more smile, please," he urged. "One more radiant smile—"

He raised the camera and lowered it again. "Er, not too radiant, dear," he told Bet, who glared at him crossly. He raised the camera again. Just as he clicked the shutter Bet put out her tongue and he lowered it hastily. His smile faded and he looked round the assembled guests.

"Whose little girl is this?" he began but the three children didn't wait to hear any more.

"She'll catch us up," said Debbie and they hurried away from the scene.

Later on they presented the flowers and a home made card to Steve's Gran, who was very pleased with them.

"That's a really nice thought," she said and she propped the card on the mantelpiece and put the flowers in water.

Then it was time to pack and rush to the station to catch the train home.

Once in the train, the children all leaned out of the window and waved 'Goodbye'. Then they settled down for the return journey.

"We sure had a good time," said Howie. "I vote we go back next year."

And the Gumby Gang agreed unanimously!

More hilarious Knight books in this series

Pamela Oldfield

THE ADVENTURES OF THE GUMBY GANG
THE GUMBY GANG AGAIN
MORE ABOUT THE GUMBY GANG

'Well written, entertaining and reassuring in the way that books for younger children ought to be.'
The Times Educational Supplement